IT'S ELECTRIC!

ELECTRIC MOTORCYCLES

Jessica Rusick

Big Buddy Books
An Imprint of Abdo Publishing
abdobooks.com

abdobooks.com

Published by Abdo Publishing, a division of ABDO, PO Box 398166, Minneapolis, Minnesota 55439.

Printed in the United States of America, North Mankato, Minnesota
052023
092023

THIS BOOK CONTAINS RECYCLED MATERIALS

Design: Sarah DeYoung, Mighty Media, Inc.
Production: Mighty Media, Inc.
Editor: Katherine Chu
Cover Photograph: Muc10/Wikimedia Commons
Interior Photographs: CJM Photography/Alamy Stock Photo, pp. 23, 24–25, 29 (LiveWire One); Daniel Hartwig/Flickr, pp. 15, 17, 18–19, 28 (LS-218); Fabrizio Annovi/Shutterstock Images, p. 27; Harley Davidson/Wikimedia Commons, pp. 21, 29 (LiveWire prototype); J2R/Shutterstock Images, p. 7; Muc10/Wikimedia Commons, pp. 11, 13; VGstockstudio/Shutterstock Images, p. 5; Zero Motorcycles Inc./Wikimedia Commons, pp. 9, 28 (Zero S)
Design Elements: octopusaga/Shutterstock Images (hexagon pattern); Vlad Malinovskij/Shutterstock Images (lightning bolt icon); Zoa.Arts/Shutterstock Images (lightning)

Library of Congress Control Number: 2022948829

Publisher's Cataloging-in-Publication Data
Names: Rusick, Jessica, author.
Title: Electric motorcycles / by Jessica Rusick
Description: Minneapolis, Minnesota : Abdo Publishing, 2024 | Series: It's electric! | Includes online resources and index.
Identifiers: ISBN 9781098291556 (lib. bdg.) | ISBN 9781098278014 (ebook)
Subjects: LCSH: Electric motorcycles--Juvenile literature. | Motorcycles--Juvenile literature. | Electric vehicles--Juvenile literature. | Transportation--Juvenile literature.
Classification: DDC 388--dc23

CONTENTS

CHAPTER 1

SMOOTH & SILENT

A motorcycle zooms down the road. The **motor** whirs quietly. But there is no engine noise or smoke. In fact, this motorcycle doesn't even have an **exhaust** pipe. That's because it's an electric **vehicle** (EV)!

FAST FACT

Electric motorcycles were invented in the early 1900s. But they were not as popular as gas-powered motorcycles, which were faster and more powerful.

Modern electric motorcycles perform better and are easier to maintain than gas-powered motorcycles.

CHAPTER 2

WHY ELECTRIC?

An EV's **motor** is powered by electricity that is stored in **rechargeable batteries**. Since the 2000s, electric motorcycles (e-motorcycles) have grown in popularity for a few reasons. Gas **vehicles release** gases that harm Earth. EVs do not. Charging an EV costs less than buying gas. And modern batteries make EVs faster and more powerful.

An e-motorcycle's batteries are charged by plugging a charger into the vehicle's charging port.

CHAPTER 3

ZERO MOTORCYCLES

Many e-motorcycle companies formed in the 2000s. In 2006, **engineer** Neil Saiki founded Zero Motorcycles.

In 2009, the company **released** its first e-motorcycle, the Zero S. It was the world's first **mass-produced** street e-motorcycle! Riders liked the Zero S's quick **acceleration** and **affordable** price. Others wished its **motor** had more power.

The 2009 Zero S had a top speed of 60 miles per hour (97 kmh). It could also travel up to 60 miles (97 km) on one charge.

In 2012, Zero Motorcycles **redesigned** the Zero S. The improved e-motorcycle was more powerful and had a new **battery** design. This gave the 2012 Zero S a faster top speed and longer range. Since then, Zero Motorcycles has continued to improve its e-motorcycle models and create new ones.

FAST FACT

Zero Motorcycles went by Electricross until 2007. The company's name changed to reflect its goal of creating zero emissions, or air pollutants.

The 2012 Zero S had a top speed of 88 miles per hour (142 kmh).

CHAPTER 4

AFFORDABLE CITY RIDING

By 2022, Zero Motorcycles was selling nine e-motorcycle models. This included a new Zero S. Upon **release**, the 2022 Zero S cost $11,195. It could drive up to 89 miles (143 km) on one charge. It also had a top speed of 98 miles per hour (158 kmh). Buyers felt the 2022 Zero S was **affordable** and great for city riding.

Zero Motorcycles makes its vehicles with aircraft-grade aluminum frames to make them lighter.

CHAPTER 5

LIGHTNING MOTORCYCLES

Like Zero Motorcycles, Lightning Motorcycles was founded in 2006. Over the next several years, the company worked to create its first e-motorcycle.

Lightning Motorcycles' model set a speed record for e-motorcycles in 2011. It reached 218 miles per hour (351 kmh)! This is why it was named the Lightning LS-218.

The LS-218 can go from 0 to 60 miles per hour (97 kmh) in 2.2 seconds.

Lightning Motorcycles started selling the LS-218 in 2014. In 2018, the company moved to a larger building. With more space, it was able to start **mass production** of the LS-218 in 2019.

In 2022, the LS-218 was still the fastest e-motorcycle in the world! In addition to its speed, riders liked that it was light and easy to control.

In 2011, the LS-218 set the Southern California Timing Association (SCTA) official world record with an average speed of 215 miles per hour (346 kmh).

LIGHTNING LS-218

Starting price: $38,888

Top speed: 218 miles per hour (351 kmh)

Range: Average of 100 miles (161 km) on one charge

Acceleration: 0 to 60 miles per hour (97 kmh) in 2.2 seconds

Charging time: 30 minutes using public fast-charging stations

Statistics from 2022 model

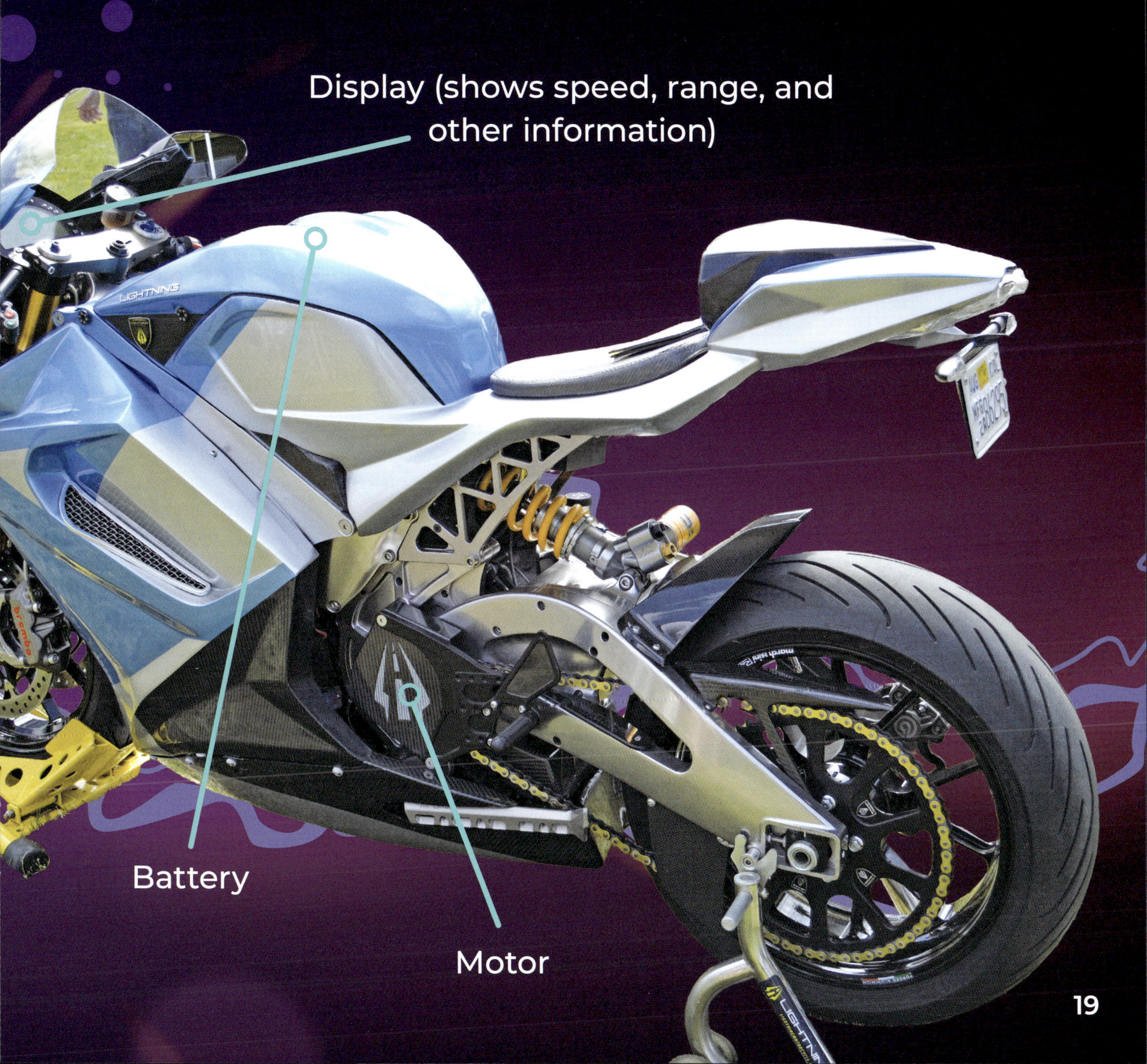
Display (shows speed, range, and other information)
Battery
Motor

CHAPTER 6

LIVEWIRE

Over time, more companies **released** new e-motorcycles. In 2014, motorcycle company Harley-Davidson created the LiveWire, its first e-motorcycle model.

The LiveWire was officially released in 2019. Buyers loved its steady ride and quick **acceleration**. But many people felt the LiveWire cost too much.

In 2019, Harley-Davidson tested its LiveWire e-motorcycle on the Formula E racetrack in Brooklyn, New York.

In 2021, Harley-Davidson **released** the LiveWire ONE. The new e-motorcycle cost less than the LiveWire. Riders felt the LiveWire ONE was an excellent bike for the price.

In 2022, LiveWire separated from Harley-Davidson and became its own company. Its goal is to continue to make **affordable** e-motorcycles.

In 2022, the Livewire ONE was featured during the Goodwood Festival of Speed in England.

LIVEWIRE ONE

Starting price: $22,799

Top speed: 110 miles per hour (177 kmh)

Range: Up to 146 miles (235 km) on one charge

Acceleration: 0 to 60 miles per hour (97 kmh) in 3 seconds

Charging time: 60 minutes using public fast-charging stations

Statistics from 2021 model

Touchscreen display (shows speed, range, and other information)
Battery
Motor

CHAPTER 7

THE FUTURE'S ELECTRIC

E-motorcycles are only beginning to rise in popularity. In the **future**, **experts** say e-motorcycle sales will keep growing. **Engineers** are also improving e-motorcycle **designs** and **batteries**.

New e-motorcycles will cost less and be more powerful. In the future, e-motorcycles may rule the road!

The Energica EGO can go as far as 261 miles (420 km) on one charge. In 2022, it had the longest range of any electric motorcycle.

TIMELINE

2006

Zero Motorcycles is founded.
Lightning Motorcycles is founded.

2011

A Lightning LS-218 sets a speed record for e-motorcycles.

2009

Zero Motorcycles **releases** the Zero S, the first **mass-produced** street e-motorcycle.

2019

The LiveWire e-motorcycle is officially **released**. The first **mass-produced** Lightning LS-218s are released.

2021

The LiveWire ONE e-motorcycle is released.

2014

Motorcycle company Harley-Davidson creates its first model e-motorcycle, the LiveWire.

2022

LiveWire becomes its own company.

GLOSSARY

acceleration (ihk-seh-luh-RAY-shuhn)—the act of increasing in speed.

affordable—having a cost that is not too high.

battery—a small container filled with chemicals that makes electrical power.

design (dih-ZINE)—to make a plan for how something will appear or work. Such a plan is called a design. To redesign something is to change its design.

engineer (ehn-juh-NIHR)—a person who is trained to apply scientific knowledge to a practical purpose such as building machines or buildings.

exhaust (ihg-ZAWST)—used gas or vapor that comes out of an engine.

expert—a person who has special skill or knowledge on a subject or activity.

future (FYOO-chuhr)—a time that has not yet occurred.

mass-produced—made in large quantities, usually by machines. This process is called mass production.

motor—a machine that produces motion or power for doing work.

recharge—to become charged again. Rechargeable means that something is able to be charged again.

release—to let go or make available to the public.

vehicle—something used for carrying persons or large objects. Some examples of vehicles are cars, trucks, boats, and airplanes.

ONLINE RESOURCES

Booklinks
NONFICTION NETWORK
FREE! ONLINE NONFICTION RESOURCES

To learn more about electric motorcycles, visit abdobooklinks.com. These links are routinely monitored and updated to provide the most current information available.

INDEX